P.L. 111-3: The Children's Health Insurance Program Reauthorization Act of 2009

Evelyne P. Baumrucker
Analyst in Health Care Financing

Elicia J. Herz
Specialist in Health Care Financing

Jane G. Gravelle
Senior Specialist in Economic Policy

January 10, 2013

Congressional Research Service

7-5700

www.crs.gov

R40226

CRS Report for Congress

Prepared for Members and Committees of Congress

Summary

The Children's Health Insurance Program Reauthorization Act of 2009 (H.R. 2, CHIPRA) was first passed in the House on January 14, 2009, and an amended version was passed in the Senate on January 29, 2009. On February 4, 2009, the House passed H.R. 2 as amended by the Senate and later that day President Obama signed the bill into law as P.L. 111-3. One of the provisions of CHIPRA permits using CHIP as the program's acronym, instead of SCHIP. This report reflects this change, using CHIP instead of SCHIP.

The overall structure of CHIPRA is similar to its two predecessors, H.R. 976 and H.R. 3963 from the 110th Congress. This report summarizes changes to prior law made by CHIPRA, and provides a brief legislative history of the major State Children's Health Insurance (CHIP) reauthorization bills in the 110th and 111th Congresses.

This report reflects the provisions at the time of CHIPRA's enactment. It is meant to serve as a historical reference to the complete set of provisions included in the law, as of February 4, 2009. It will not be updated to capture subsequent legislative changes, program guidance, public notices, or rulemaking. During the 112th Congress, The American Taxpayer Relief Act (ATRA, P.L. 112-240) extended the state option for "Express Lane" eligibility to conduct simplified eligibility determinations for Medicaid and CHIP children for an additional 12 months, through September 30, 2014. No other legislative changes were made to the CHIP program during the 112th Congress. (For information on changes to the State Children's Health Insurance Program enacted under the Patient Protection and Affordable Care Act [ACA; P.L. 111-148, as amended], see CRS Report R41210, *Medicaid and the State Children's Health Insurance Program (CHIP) Provisions in ACA: Summary and Timeline.*)

Contents

Tables

Appendixes

Contacts

Background

The Balanced Budget Act of 1997 (P.L. 105-33, BBA-97) established the State Children's Health Insurance Program (CHIP) under a new Title XXI of the Social Security Act. CHIP builds on Medicaid by providing health care coverage to low-income, uninsured children in families with incomes above applicable Medicaid income standards. The latest official numbers show that CHIP enrollment reached a total of nearly 7.4 million children and nearly 335,000 adults in FY2008. In FY2008, federal CHIP spending totaled $7.0 billion, with states' projected spending expected to equal $7.9 billion in FY2009.

In BBA 97, Congress authorized and appropriated funds for FY1998-FY2007, with no federal appropriations slated for FY2008 and beyond. The absence of future federal appropriations triggered CHIP legislative attention during the 110th Congress. One of the first acts of the 111th Congress was to reauthorize the program. On February 4, 2009, President Obama signed the Children's Health Insurance Program Reauthorization Act of 2009 (P.L. 111-3, CHIPRA) into law. This report summarizes the changes to prior law made by CHIPRA, including

- a national appropriation for CHIP allotments totaling $68.9 billion over five years, distributed to states and territories using a new formula primarily based on their past and/or projected federal CHIP spending. For FY2009 onward, annual allotments would be available for two years, with unspent funds available for redistribution first to shortfall states and then toward bonus payments, described below.[1]

- a new contingency fund (for making payments to states for certain shortfalls of federal CHIP funds), which receives deposits through a separate appropriation each year through FY2013, and makes payments of up to 20% of the available national allotment for CHIP for each eligible shortfall state;

- new performance bonus payments (for states exceeding certain child enrollment levels and states that implement certain outreach and enrollment initiatives), which are funded with a FY2009 appropriation of $3.225 billion and deposits of certain unspent CHIP funds through FY2013;

- additional grants for outreach and enrollment totaling $100 million each year through FY2013;

- provisions to remove barriers to enrollment including a state option to rely on findings from specified "Express Lane" agencies for eligibility determinations in Medicaid and CHIP;

- a state option to extend coverage to pregnant women under CHIP through a state plan amendment when certain conditions are met;

- provisions to terminate CHIP adult coverage waivers, and establish conditions to continue existing waivers under Medicaid;

---

[1] Cost estimates from the Congressional Budget Office (CBO) indicated that CHIPRA would increase overall outlays (across all provisions of the bill) by $32.8 billion over five years (FY2009-13), which would be offset primarily by increases in federal tobacco taxes, estimated to increase on-budget revenue by $32.8 billion over five years.

- a state option to waive the five-year bar for Medicaid or SCHIP coverage to pregnant women and children who are lawfully residing in the United States and are otherwise eligible for such coverage;

- provisions to provide a specific alternative for states to verify proof of citizenship, and a requirement for citizenship documentation in SCHIP;

- provisions related to benefits (e.g., dental, mental health);

- a state plan option for premium assistance to enroll in employer-based health insurance, and elimination of barriers to providing premium assistance;

- provisions to strengthen quality of care and health outcomes of children;

- a Medicaid and CHIP Payment and Access Commission;

- program integrity and miscellaneous provisions, including some that affect the Medicaid program; and

- tobacco tax changes.

The overall structure of CHIPRA is similar to its two predecessors, H.R. 976 and H.R. 3963 from the 110th Congress. The **Appendix** provides a summary of the major CHIP legislation during the 110th and 111th Congresses.

The Children's Health Insurance Program Reauthorization Act of 2009 (CHIPRA)

The Children's Health Insurance Program Reauthorization Act of 2009 (CHIPRA, H.R. 2) was passed in the House on January 14, 2009, and an amended version was passed in the Senate on January 29, 2009.[2] On February 4, 2009, the House passed H.R. 2 (as amended by the Senate), and later that day President Obama signed the bill into law as P.L. 111-3, the Children's Health Insurance Program Reauthorization Act of 2009 (CHIPRA). One of the provisions of CHIPRA permits using CHIP as the program's acronym, instead of SCHIP. This report reflects this change, using CHIP instead of SCHIP.

CHIPRA is effective April 1, 2009, which is the beginning of the second half of the federal fiscal year. States will be given additional time to come into compliance with the requirements of CHIPRA, if applicable, based on the timing of state legislative sessions. If FY2009 CHIP allotment amounts provided for the first two quarters of FY2009 have not been obligated, they will be rescinded and will effectively be replaced with funding provided in this act. The amount of allotments provided under CHIPRA in the second half of FY2009 will be reduced by spending that occurred from a state's FY2009 allotment in the first half of the fiscal year. Provisions in the act will be considered effective on the dates specified regardless of whether implementing regulations have been issued. In addition, states cannot be denied Medicaid and CHIP payments if

---

[2] The Senate Finance Committee ordered reported its version of CHIPRA on January 15, 2009, which was then introduced for Senate floor consideration as S. 275. The Senate then took up H.R. 2 as passed by the House and replaced it with language from S. 275 (S.Amdt. 39 to H.R. 2). The Senate then passed six additional amendments.

they acted in good faith reliance on the provisions of the act, even if those expenditures do not comply with the final regulations ultimately issued.

Cost estimates from the Congressional Budget Office (CBO) indicated that CHIPRA would increase outlays by $32.8 billion over 5 years and by $66.1 billion over 10 years. Those costs would be offset primarily by increases in federal tobacco taxes, which were estimated to increase on-budget revenue by $32.8 billion over 5 years and by $66.6 billion over 10 years.[3]

On any given day in 2007, approximately 9 million children were without health insurance. Most of these children came from two-parent families (53%). Most had a parent who worked full time all year (60%).[4] And other data indicate most uninsured children are *eligible* for Medicaid or CHIP (62%).[5] CBO estimated CHIPRA will increase average monthly FY2013 Medicaid and CHIP enrollment by 6.5 million over prior-law estimates, for a total of 37.7 million projected enrollees. About 80% of the increased enrollment would occur among current eligibility groups, rather than new ones. Of the 6.5 million increased average monthly enrollment in FY2013, CBO estimates that 2.4 million (37%) would have private coverage in the absence of the legislation and that 4.1 million (63%) would be uninsured.

The overall structure of CHIPRA is similar to its two predecessors, H.R. 976 and H.R. 3963 from the 110th Congress. The remainder of this report summarizes changes to prior law as enacted by CHIPRA.

This report reflects the provisions at the time of CHIPRA's enactment. It is meant to serve as an historical reference to the complete set of provisions included in the law, as of February 4, 2009. It will not be updated to capture subsequent legislative changes, program guidance, public notices, or rulemaking. During the 112th Congress, *The American Taxpayer Relief Act* (ATRA, P.L. 112-240) extended the state option for "Express Lane" eligibility determinations for Medicaid and CHIP children through September 30, 2014. No other legislative changes were made to the CHIP program during the 112th Congress. (For information on changes to the State Children's Health Insurance Program enacted under the Patient Protection and Affordable Care Act [ACA; P.L. 111-148, as amended], see CRS Report R41210, *Medicaid and the State Children's Health Insurance Program (CHIP) Provisions in ACA: Summary and Timeline.*)

---

[3] Congressional Budget Office cost estimate, "H.R. 2, Children's Health Insurance Program Reauthorization Act of 2009," February 11, 2009, available at http://www.cbo.gov/ftpdocs/99xx/doc9985/hr2paygo.pdf.

[4] CRS Report 97-975, *Health Insurance Coverage of Children, 2008.*

[5] Julie L. Hudson and Thomas M. Selden, "Children's Eligibility And Coverage: Recent Trends And A Look Ahead," Health Affairs Web exclusive, August 16, 2007, pp. w618-629.

Summary of Provisions in P.L. 111-3

TITLE I-FINANCING

Subtitle A-Funding

Sections 101. Extension of CHIP.

Under prior law, BBA97 created the Children's Health Insurance Program (CHIP) and appropriated $40 billion for CHIP original allotments from FY1998 to FY2007.

The Medicare, Medicaid, and CHIP Extension Act of 2007 (MMSEA, P.L. 110-173) appropriated allotments and additional funding to prevent any state from running out of federal CHIP funds before March 31, 2009. The CHIP appropriation for original allotments in FY2007, the last year provided for in BBA97, totaled $5.04 billion. MMSEA provided that same amount annually for CHIP allotments in FY2008 and FY2009, stating, however, that these funds "shall not be available for child health assistance [CHIP expenditures] for items and services furnished after March 31, 2009." MMSEA also provided up to $275 million to cover any shortfalls of federal CHIP funds for the first half of FY2009—that is, through March 31, 2009.

CHIPRA provides national appropriations for CHIP allotments as follows:

- $10.562 billion in FY2009;
- $12.52 billion in FY2010;
- $13.459 billion in FY2011;
- $14.982 billion in FY2012; and
- $2.85 billion for the first half of FY2013 and $2.85 billion for the second half of FY2013. See "Section 108. One-time appropriation." for additional FY2013 CHIP funding.

Section 102. Allotments for States and territories for fiscal years 2009 through 2013.

Prior to CHIPRA, of the national appropriation ($5 billion for each of FY2007, FY2008 and FY2009, for example), the territories receive 0.25%. The remainder ($4.9875 billion for each of FY2007, FY2008 and FY2009) was divided, or allotted, among the states based on a formula using survey estimates of the number of low-income children in the state and the number of those children who were uninsured. These amounts were adjusted by a geographic adjustment factor and were limited by various floors and ceilings to ensure that a state's allotment did not vary substantially from certain past allotments.

Rather than dividing a fixed national appropriation on the basis of state survey estimates, CHIPRA calculates a state's allotment as described below—and if the total of all the states' and territories' allotments does not exceed the national appropriation, that will be the state's allotment.

FY2009 Allotment

FY2009 federal CHIP allotments for states under CHIPRA will be based on the largest of three state-specific amounts:

- the state's FY2008 federal CHIP spending, multiplied by a growth factor;
- the state's FY2008 federal CHIP allotment, multiplied by a growth factor; and
- the state's own projections of federal CHIP spending for FY2009, submitted by states to the Secretary of Health and Human Services (HHS) as of February 2009.

The largest of these three amounts will be increased by 10% and will serve as the state's FY2009 federal CHIP allotment, as long as the national appropriation is adequate to cover all the states' and territories' FY2009 allotments. If not, allotments will be reduced proportionally.

FY2010 Allotment

For FY2010, the allotment for a state (or territory) will be calculated as the sum of the following four amounts, if applicable, multiplied by the applicable growth factor for the year:

- the FY2009 CHIP allotment;
- FY2006 unspent allotments redistributed to and spent by shortfall states in FY2009;
- Spending of funds provided to shortfall states in the first half of FY2009; and
- Spending of Contingency Fund payments (discussed below) in FY2009, although there may be none.

FY2011 and FY2013 Allotments

For FY2011 and FY2013, the allotment for a state (or territory) will be "rebased," based on prior year spending. This will be done by multiplying the state's growth factor for the year by the new base, which will be the prior year's federal CHIP spending from allotments, redistribution, and Contingency Fund payments.

FY2012 Allotment

For FY2012, the allotment for a state (or territory) will be calculated as the FY2011 allotment and any FY2011 Contingency Fund spending, multiplied by the state's growth factor for the year.

Section 103. Child Enrollment Contingency Fund.

A Child Enrollment Contingency Fund will be established and funded initially by a separate appropriation of 20% of the available national allotment for CHIP in FY2009 (approximately $2.1 billion). For FY2010 through FY2013, the appropriation will be such sums as are necessary for making payments to eligible states for the fiscal year, as long as the annual payments do not exceed 20% of that fiscal year's available national CHIP allotment.

If a state's federal CHIP spending in FY2009 through FY2013 exceeds its available allotments (excluding unspent allotments redistributed from other states) and if the state experiences enrollment that exceeded its target average number (FY2008 enrollment plus annual state child population growth plus one percentage point per year), payments from the Contingency Fund will be the projected federal CHIP costs for those enrollees above the target number in the state.

Section 104. CHIP performance bonus payment to offset additional enrollment costs resulting from enrollment and retention efforts.

Funds for bonus payments will be payable in FY2009 to FY2013 to states that increase their Medicaid (not CHIP) enrollment among low-income children above a defined baseline. To qualify for bonus payments, states will also have to implement five of the following eight outreach and enrollment activities:

- 12 months of continuous eligibility for Medicaid and CHIP children;
- Elimination of an assets test in Medicaid and CHIP, or use of administrative verification of assets;
- Elimination of in-person interview requirement;
- Use of a joint application for Medicaid and CHIP;
- Implementation of certain options to ease enrollees' renewal processes;
- Presumptive eligibility for children;
- Implementation of "Express Lane," described in Section 203; and
- Implementation of premium assistance, described in Section 301.

The payments would be funded by an initial appropriation in FY2009 of $3.225 billion, along with transfers from four different potential sources:

- National appropriation amounts for FY2009 through FY2013 provided but not used for allotments;
- Redistribution amounts not spent; and
- On October 1 of FY2010 through FY2013, any amounts in the CHIP Contingency Fund that exceed its cap (described above).[6]

For FY2009, the Medicaid bonus baseline is equal to the state's average monthly number of enrolled Medicaid children in 2007, increased by state child population growth between 2007 and 2008 (estimated by the U.S. Census Bureau) plus four percentage points, further increased by state child population growth between 2008 and 2009 plus four percentage points. For subsequent years, the Medicaid bonus baseline is the prior year's number plus state child population growth

---

[6] An additional category included in CHIPRA reflects earlier versions of the legislation, pointing to unspent amounts in the transitional coverage block grant for non-pregnant childless adults. However, such a block grant was not included in the final version of CHIPRA.

plus additional percentage point increases that are lower than the 4 percentage points for FY2009: for FY2010 to FY2012, 3.5 percentage points; for FY2013 to FY2015, 3 percentage points; and FY2016 onward, 2 percentage points.

The first tier of bonus payments is for child Medicaid enrollees that represent growth above the baseline less than 10%. For these Medicaid child enrollees, the bonus payment is equal to 15% of the state share of these enrollees' projected per capita Medicaid expenditures. (Projected per capita Medicaid expenditures are the average per capita Medicaid expenditures for children for the most recent year with actual data, increased by necessary projected annual increases in per capita National Health Expenditures.) For the second tier, 10% or more above baseline, the bonus payment is 62.5% of the state share of these enrollees' projected per capita expenditures.

An eligibility expansion would not qualify a state for additional bonus payments. In order for new Medicaid children to count toward bonus payments, they must have been able to meet the state's eligibility criteria in place on July 1, 2008.

If the available funding for bonus payments to states in a given year is inadequate, the payments would be reduced proportionally.

Under prior law, a number of entities may make Medicaid "presumptive eligibility" determinations for children (e.g., medical providers, entities that determine eligibility for Head Start). Presumptive eligibility allows children who appear to be eligible for Medicaid based on an initial determination to be enrolled for up to two months of coverage while a final determination of eligibility is made. Children who were enrolled in Medicaid through presumptive eligibility would only count for a state's bonus payments if the child was ultimately enrolled through a final determination.

Section 105. Two-year initial availability of CHIP allotments.

Although federal CHIP allotments under BBA97 were made available for three years, allotments for FY2009 onward under CHIPRA would be available for two years.

Section 106. Redistribution of unused allotments.

Under CHIPRA, unspent funds available for redistribution would first be provided to shortfall states and then, if any remain, toward bonus payments.

Section 107. Option for States to receive the enhanced portion of the CHIP matching rate for Medicaid coverage of certain children.

Under BBA97, states faced a maintenance of effort so they could not draw federal CHIP funds for child populations already covered under Medicaid. States that had expanded Medicaid coverage to higher income children prior to CHIP expressed that this was a penalty against their early expansion efforts. A provision was added later in CHIP to permit 11 early expansion "qualifying states"[7] to draw some CHIP funds for Medicaid children above 150% of poverty, although with

---

[7] Connecticut, Hawaii, Maryland, Minnesota, New Hampshire, New Mexico, Rhode Island, Tennessee, Vermont, Washington and Wisconsin.

an additional limit in the amount besides just their available federal CHIP funds (that is, no more than 20% from each original allotment could be spent on these Medicaid children).

CHIPRA would permit this spending for Medicaid children above *133%* of poverty, and without the 20% limitation.

Section 108. One-time appropriation.

A "one-time appropriation" of $11.706 billion will be added to the half-year amounts provided for FY2013 described in Section 101. These provisions for FY2013 are intended to annually reduce by the "one-time appropriation" the amount of allotments assumed by the Congressional Budget Office (CBO) for fiscal years after FY2013.

Subtitle B-Focus on Low-Income Children and Pregnant Women

Section 111. State option to cover low-income pregnant women under CHIP through a State plan amendment.

Under prior CHIP law, states were permitted to cover pregnant women ages 19 and older through waiver authority or by providing coverage to unborn children as permitted through regulation. In the latter case, coverage is supposed to be limited to prenatal and delivery services. CHIPRA allows states to cover pregnant women under CHIP through a state plan amendment when certain conditions are met (e.g., the Medicaid income standard for pregnant women must be at least 185% FPL but in no case lower than the percentage level in effect on July 1, 2008; no pre-existing conditions or waiting periods may be imposed; CHIP cost-sharing protections apply). The upper income limit may be as high as the standard applicable to CHIP children in the state. Other eligibility restrictions applicable to CHIP children (e.g., must be uninsured, ineligible for state employee health coverage, etc.) also apply. The period of coverage is during pregnancy through the postpartum period (roughly through 60 days postpartum). States are allowed to temporarily enroll pregnant women for up to two months until a formal determination of eligibility is made. Benefits include all services available to CHIP children in the state as well as prenatal, delivery, and postpartum care. Infants born to these pregnant women are deemed eligible for Medicaid or CHIP, as appropriate, and are covered up to age one year. States may continue to cover pregnant women through waivers and the unborn child regulation. In the latter case, states are allowed to offer postpartum services.

Section 112. Phase-out of coverage for nonpregnant childless adults under CHIP; conditions for coverage of parents.

Under current law, Section 1115 of the Social Security Act gives the Secretary of Health and Human Services (HHS) broad authority to modify many aspects of the Medicaid and CHIP programs including expanding eligibility to populations who are not otherwise eligible for Medicaid or CHIP (e.g., childless adults, pregnant women age 19 and older, and parents of Medicaid and CHIP-eligible children). Certain states that have covered adults with CHIP funds were permitted to do so almost entirely through the use of these waivers. Adult coverage waivers, which initially are effective for five years, are subject to renewal at least every three years. Prior to 2007, waiver renewals for states with adult coverage waivers were approved, even for those states that were projected to face federal CHIP shortfalls (e.g., New Jersey, Rhode Island).

Beginning in 2007, however, such waiver renewals have not been approved (e.g., Illinois, Oregon) or states have begun to transition adult populations out of CHIP coverage (e.g., Wisconsin, Minnesota). As of January 7, 2009, four states have CMS authority to use CHIP funds to extend coverage to certain childless adult populations, and seven states have such authority to cover parent populations.

CHIPRA terminates CHIP coverage of nonpregnant childless adults by the end of calendar year 2009. States with existing childless adult waivers are permitted to apply for Medicaid waivers to continue coverage for these individuals subject to a specified budget neutrality standard, but in FY2010 childless adult spending under the waiver will be tied to the state's 2009 waiver spending on this population. CHIPRA requires budget neutrality standards for succeeding fiscal years to be tied to waiver spending in the preceding fiscal year.

Under CHIPRA, coverage of parents is allowed, but beginning in FY2012, allowable spending under the waivers will be subject to a set-aside amount from a separate allotment and will be matched at the state's regular Medicaid FMAP unless the state was able to prove it met certain coverage benchmarks (related to performance in providing coverage to children). In FY2013, even states meeting the coverage benchmarks will not get the enhanced FMAP for parents but an amount between the regular and enhanced FMAPs. Finally, the provision prohibits waiver spending under the set-aside for parents whose family income exceeds the income eligibility thresholds that were in effect under the existing waivers as of the date of enactment of CHIPRA.

Section 113. Elimination of counting Medicaid child presumptive eligibility costs against title XXI.

Prior SCHIP statute set the federal share of costs incurred during periods of presumptive eligibility for Medicaid children (i.e., up to two months of coverage while a final determination of eligibility is made) at the Medicaid matching rate. Prior law also allowed payment out of SCHIP allotments for Medicaid benefits received by Medicaid children during periods of presumptive eligibility. A number of entities may make presumptive eligibility determinations for children (e.g., medical providers, entities that determine eligibility for Head Start, and for a special supplemental nutrition program for women, infants and children or WIC). A provision in CHIPRA eliminates the counting of Medicaid child presumptive eligibility costs against state SCHIP allotments, and allows entities that make presumptive eligibility determinations for children under Medicaid to make such determinations for pregnant women under Medicaid.

Under prior Medicaid law, newborns were deemed eligible for coverage through age 1 as long as they remained in the mother's household and the mother remained eligible for Medicaid during this period. A provision in CHIPRA provides continuous eligibility of newborns through age 1, regardless of the living arrangements and mothers' eligibility.

Section 114. Limitation on matching rate for States that propose to cover children with effective family income that exceeds 300 percent of the poverty line.

The federal medical assistance percentage (FMAP) is the state-specific percentage of Medicaid service expenditures paid by the federal government. It is based on a formula that provides higher reimbursement rates to states with lower per capita incomes relative to the national average (and vice versa); it has a statutory minimum of 50% and maximum of 83%. The enhanced FMAP (E-

FMAP) for CHIP reduces the state's share under the regular FMAP by 30%. The E-FMAP has a statutory minimum of 65% and maximum of 85%.

CHIPRA reduces federal CHIP payments for certain higher-income CHIP children. It specifies that the regular FMAP would be used for CHIP enrollees whose effective family income exceeds 300% of poverty using the state's policy of excluding "a block of income that is not determined by type of expense or type of income," with an exception for states that already had a federal approval plan or that had enacted a state law to submit a plan for federal approval.

Section 115. State authority under Medicaid.

Under prior law, children in a Medicaid-expansion CHIP program were to be paid for out of CHIP funds at the E-FMAP. Medicaid funding for these children could not be used until a state's available CHIP funding was exhausted. CHIPRA gives states the option to draw Medicaid funds at the regular FMAP for Medicaid-expansion CHIP children.

TITLE II-OUTREACH AND ENROLLMENT

Subtitle A-Outreach and Enrollment Activities

Section 201. Grants and enhanced administrative funding for outreach and enrollment.

CHIPRA authorizes $100 million in outreach and enrollment grants above and beyond the regular CHIP allotments for fiscal years 2009 through 2013. Ten percent of the allocation will be directed to a national enrollment campaign, and 10% will be targeted to outreach for Native American children. The remaining 80% will be distributed among state and local governments and to community-based organizations for purposes of conducting outreach campaigns with a particular focus on rural areas and underserved populations. Grant funds will also be targeted at proposals that address cultural and linguistic barriers to enrollment. CHIP includes outreach to Native Americans as a part of the National Enrollment Campaign.

Section 202. Increased outreach and enrollment of Indians.

Under prior SCHIP law, state SCHIP plans were required to include a description of procedures used to ensure the provision of child health assistance to American Indian and Alaskan Native children. Also, certain non-benefit payments under SCHIP (e.g., for other child health assistance, health service initiatives, outreach and program administration) cannot exceed 10% of the total amount of expenditures for benefits and these non-benefit payments combined.

A provision in CHIPRA encourages states to take steps to enroll Indians residing in or near reservations in Medicaid and CHIP. These steps may include outstationing eligibility workers; entering into agreements with Indian entities (i.e., the IHS, tribes, tribal organizations) to provide outreach; education regarding eligibility, benefits, and enrollment; and translation services. The Secretary must facilitate cooperation between states and Indian entities in providing benefits to Indians under Medicaid and CHIP. This provision also excludes costs for outreach to potentially eligible Indian children and families from the 10% cap on non-benefit expenditures under CHIP.

Section 203. State option to rely on findings from an Express Lane agency to conduct simplified eligibility determinations.[8]

CHIPRA creates a state option to rely on a finding from specified "Express Lane" agencies (e.g., those that administer programs such as Temporary Assistance for Needy Families, Medicaid, CHIP, and Food Stamps) to determine whether a child under age 19 (or an age specified by the state not to exceed 21 years of age) has met one or more of the eligibility requirements (e.g., income, assets or resources, citizenship, or other criteria) necessary to determine an individual's initial eligibility, eligibility redetermination, or renewal of eligibility for medical assistance under Medicaid or CHIP. States will have the option to institute automatic enrollment through an Express Lane eligibility determination contingent on a family's signature of consent, or consent obtained in writing, by telephone, orally, through electronic signature, or any other means specified by the Secretary of HHS. The provision gives states the option to rely on an applicant's reported income as shown by state income tax records or returns. Under CHIPRA, states are required to inform families that they may qualify for lower premium payments or more comprehensive health coverage under Medicaid if the family's income were directly evaluated by the state Medicaid agency. CHIPRA also drops the requirement for signatures on a Medicaid or CHIP application form under penalty of perjury.

Subtitle B-Reducing Barriers to Enrollment

Section 211. Verification of declaration of citizenship or nationality for purposes of eligibility for Medicaid and CHIP.

The Deficit Reduction Act of 2005 (DRA) requires citizens and nationals applying for Medicaid who claim to be citizens to provide both proof of citizenship and identity. Before DRA, states could accept self-declaration of citizenship for Medicaid, although some chose to require additional supporting evidence. CHIPRA provides a specific alternative, which allows a state to use the Social Security Number (SSN) provided by individuals and verified by the Social Security Administration (SSA), and provides an enhanced match for certain administrative costs. (SSNs by themselves do not denote citizenship, because certain noncitizens are eligible for them.) CHIPRA also adds a requirement for citizenship documentation in CHIP.

Section 212. Reducing administrative barriers to enrollment.

During the implementation of CHIP, states instituted a variety of enrollment facilitation and outreach strategies to bring eligible children into Medicaid and CHIP. As a result, substantial progress was made at the state level to simplify the application and enrollment processes to find, enroll, and maintain eligibility among those eligible for the program. CHIPRA requires the state plan to describe the procedures used to reduce the administrative barriers to the enrollment of children and pregnant women in Medicaid and CHIP, and to ensure that such procedures are revised as often as the state determines is appropriate to reduce newly identified barriers to

---

[8] During the 112th Congress, The American Taxpayer Relief Act (ATRA, P.L. 112-240) extended the period through which states can rely on "Express Lane" eligibility determinations to determine whether a child has met one or more of the eligibility requirements necessary to determine an individual's eligibility for medical assistance under Medicaid or CHIP. P.L. 112-240 permits states to rely on "Express Lane" eligibility determinations through September 30, 2014.

enrollment. States will be deemed to be in compliance with these requirements if they implement joint Medicaid and CHIP application and renewal processes, and drop requirements for face-to-face interviews.

Section 213. Model of Interstate coordinated enrollment coverage process.

CHIPRA requires the Secretary of HHS, in consultation with state Medicaid, CHIP directors, and organizations representing program beneficiaries to develop a model process (and report for Congress) for the coordination of enrollment, retention, and coverage of children who frequently change their residency due to migration of families, emergency evacuations, educational needs, etc.

Section 214. Permitting States to ensure coverage without a 5-year delay of certain children and pregnant women under the Medicaid program and CHIP.

Under prior law, legal immigrants arriving in the United States after August 22, 1996, were ineligible for Medicaid or CHIP benefits for their first five years here. Coverage of such persons after the five-year bar was permitted at state option if they met other eligibility requirements for that program. For legal immigrants (but not refugees and asylees), the law requires that their sponsor's income and resources would be taken into account in determining eligibility for those who have signed a legally binding affidavit of support. Generally speaking, for federally means-tested programs (e.g., Medicaid, TANF), the affidavit of support required the sponsor to ensure that the new immigrant will not become a public charge and makes the sponsor financially responsible for the individual.

CHIPRA permits states to waive the five-year bar for Medicaid or CHIP coverage to pregnant women and children who are (1) lawfully residing in the United States and (2) are otherwise eligible for such coverage. The CHIP state plan option made available under this provision is available only to states that (1) elect this state plan option under Medicaid and (2) in the case of pregnant women coverage, elect the CHIP state plan option to provide assistance for pregnant women. For states that elect to extend such coverage, the provision assures that the cost of care will not be deemed under an affidavit of support against an individual's sponsor. In addition, as a part of states' redetermination processes (i.e., to redetermine eligibility at least every 12 months with respect to circumstances that may change and affect eligibility), individuals made eligible under this provision whose initial documentation showing legal residence is no longer valid will be required to show "further documentation or other evidence" that the individual continues to lawfully reside.

TITLE III-REDUCING BARRIERS TO PROVIDING PREMIUM ASSISTANCE

Subtitle A-Additional State Option for Providing Premium Assistance

Section 301. Additional State option for providing premium assistance.

Under prior law, states were permitted to pay a beneficiary's share of costs for group (employer-based) health insurance in CHIP if the employer plan was cost effective relative to the amount paid to cover only the targeted low-income children, and did not substitute for coverage under group health plans otherwise being provided to the children. In addition, states using CHIP funds for employer-based plan premiums were required to ensure that CHIP minimum benefits were provided and CHIP cost-sharing ceilings were met. Under Medicaid, including a Medicaid expansion CHIP program, states may implement a premium assistance program if the employer plan is comprehensive and cost-effective for the state. Under Medicaid, an individual's enrollment in an employer plan is considered cost-effective if paying the premiums, deductible, coinsurance, and other cost-sharing obligations of the employer plan is less expensive than the state's expected cost of directly providing Medicaid-covered services. To meet the comprehensiveness test under Medicaid, states are required to provide coverage for those Medicaid-covered services that are not included in the private plans. In other words, they must provide "wrap-around" benefit coverage. It has proved prohibitive for many employer plans and states to meet all of these requirements. To circumvent these restrictions, most states operating CHIP or Medicaid premium assistance programs do so under waivers.

CHIPRA creates a new state plan option for providing premium assistance. States have the option to offer premium assistance for Medicaid and CHIP-eligible children and/or parents of Medicaid and/or CHIP-eligible children where the family has access to employer-sponsored insurance (ESI) coverage, if the employer pays at least 40% of the total premium (and meets certain other requirements). Under CHIPRA, a state offering premium assistance may not require CHIP-eligible individuals to enroll in an employer's plan; individuals eligible for CHIP and for employment-based coverage may choose to enroll in regular CHIP rather than the premium assistance program. The premium assistance subsidy will generally be the difference between the worker's out-of-pocket premium that included the child(ren) versus only covering the employee. For employer plans that do not meet CHIP benefit requirements, a wrap-around is required.

For the child's coverage using premium assistance, no cost-effectiveness test is required regarding the cost of the private coverage (plus any necessary wrap-around) relative to regular CHIP coverage. CHIPRA establishes a separate test for family coverage. If the CHIP cost of covering the entire family in the employer-sponsored plan is less than regular CHIP coverage for the eligible individual(s) alone, then the premium assistance subsidy may be used to pay the entire family's share of the premium. In states that offered premium assistance, CHIPRA requires states and participating employers to do outreach. Finally, states are permitted to establish an employer-family premium assistance purchasing pool for employers with less than 250 employees who have at least one employee who is a CHIP-eligible pregnant woman or at least one member of the family is a CHIP-eligible child. Finally, the new premium assistance provisions under Medicaid, not CHIP, will apply to children enrolled in a Medicaid-expansion CHIP program.

Section 302. Outreach, education, and enrollment assistance.

CHIP state plans are required to include a description of the procedures in place to provide outreach to children eligible for CHIP child health assistance, or other public or private health programs to (1) inform these families of the availability of public and private health coverage and (2) to assist them in enrolling such children in CHIP. There is a limit on federal spending for CHIP administrative expenses (i.e., 10% of a state's spending on benefit coverage in a given fiscal year). Administrative expenses include activities such as data collection and reporting, as well as outreach and education. In addition, states are required to provide a description of the state's efforts to ensure coordination between CHIP and other health insurance coverage applies to State administrative expenses.

CHIPRA requires states to include a description of the procedures in place to provide outreach, education, and enrollment assistance for families of children likely to be eligible for premium assistance subsidies under CHIP, or a waiver approved under Section 1115. For employers likely to provide qualified employer-sponsored coverage, the state is required to include the specific resources the state intends to use to educate employers about the availability of premium assistance subsidies under the CHIP state plan. Expenditures for such outreach activities will be limited to 1.25% of the state's limit on spending for administrative costs associated with their CHIP program (i.e., 10% of the state's spending on benefit coverage in a given fiscal year).

Subtitle B-Coordinating Premium Assistance with Private Coverage

Section 311. Special enrollment period under group health plans in case of termination of Medicaid or CHIP coverage or eligibility for assistance in purchase of employment-based coverage; coordination of coverage.

Under the Internal Revenue Code, the Employee Retirement Income Security Act, and the Public Health Service Act, a group health plan is required to provide special enrollment opportunities to qualified individuals. Such individuals must have lost eligibility for other group coverage, or lost employer contributions towards health coverage, or added a dependent due to marriage, birth, adoption, or placement for adoption, in order to enroll in a group health plan without having to wait until a late enrollment opportunity or open season. The individual still must meet the plan's substantive eligibility requirements, such as being a full-time worker or satisfying a waiting period. Health plans must give qualified individuals at least 30 days after the qualifying event (e.g., loss of eligibility) to make a request for special enrollment.

CHIPRA amends applicable federal laws to streamline coordination between public and private coverage, including making the loss of Medicaid/CHIP eligibility a "qualifying event" for the purpose of purchasing employer-sponsored coverage. Individuals may request such coverage up to 60 days after the qualifying event. The provision also requires health plan administrators to disclose to the state, upon request, information about their benefit packages so states can evaluate the need to provide wraparound coverage. CHIPRA also requires employers to notify families of their potential eligibility for premium assistance.

TITLE IV-STRENGTHENING QUALITY OF CARE AND HEALTH OUTCOMES

Section 401. Child health quality improvement activities for children enrolled in Medicaid or CHIP.

CHIPRA includes several provisions designed to improve the quality of care under Medicaid and CHIP. This new law directs the Secretary of HHS to develop (1) child health quality measures, and (2) a standardized format for reporting information, and procedures to encourage states to voluntarily report on the quality of pediatric care in these two programs. Examples of these initiatives include (1) grants and contracts to develop, test, update and disseminate evidence-based measures; (2) demonstrations to evaluate promising ideas for improving the quality of children's health care under Medicaid and CHIP; (3) a demonstration to develop a comprehensive and systematic model for reducing child obesity; and (4) a program to encourage the creation and dissemination of a model electronic health record format for children enrolled in these two programs. The federal share of the costs association with developing or modifying existing state data systems to store and report child health measures is based on the matching rate applicable to benefits rather than one of the (typically) lower matching rates applied to different types of administrative expenses.

Section 402. Improved availability of public information regarding enrollment of children in CHIP and Medicaid.

CHIPRA improves the availability of public information regarding enrollment of children in Medicaid and CHIP. Several reporting requirements are added to states' annual CHIP reports, including for example, data on eligibility criteria, access to primary and specialty care, and data on premium assistance for employer-sponsored coverage. CHIPRA also requires the Secretary to improve the timeliness of the enrollment and eligibility data for Medicaid and CHIP children contained in the Medicaid Statistical Information System (MSIS) maintained by CMS and based on annual state reported enrollment and claims data. GAO must conduct a study of children's access to primary and specialty care under Medicaid and CHIP. A report on this analysis, including recommendations addressing identified barriers, is due within two years of the date of enactment.

Section 403. Application of certain managed care quality safeguards to CHIP.

Under CHIPRA, certain managed care safeguards applicable to Medicaid (e.g., process for enrollment, termination, and change in enrollment; form and substance of information available to enrollees and potential enrollees; beneficiary protections; quality assurance standards) also apply in the same manner to CHIP. This provision applies to contract years for health plans beginning on or after July 1, 2009.

TITLE V-IMPROVING ACCESS TO BENEFITS

Under current law, states may provide CHIP coverage under their Medicaid programs, create a new separate CHIP program, or both. Under separate CHIP programs, states may elect any of three benefit options: (1) a benchmark plan, (2) a benchmark-equivalent plan, or (3) any other plan that the Secretary of HHS deems would provide appropriate coverage for the target population (Secretary-approved coverage). Benchmark plans include (1) the standard Blue Cross/Blue Shield preferred provider option under the Federal Employees Health Benefits Program (FEHBP), (2) the coverage generally available to state employees, and (3) the coverage offered by the largest commercial HMO in the state. Benchmark-equivalent plans must cover basic benefits (i.e., inpatient and outpatient hospital services, physician services, lab/x-ray, and well-child care including immunizations), and must include at least 75% of the actuarial value of coverage under the selected benchmark plan for specific additional benefits (i.e., prescription drugs, mental health services, vision care, and hearing services).

CHIPRA adds or modifies several benefits available to children under CHIP. It also addresses payment of premiums and related sanctions.

Section 501. Dental benefits.

Under CHIPRA, dental services become a required benefit under CHIP and include services necessary to prevent disease and promote oral health, restore oral structures to health and function, and treat emergency conditions. States have the option to provide dental services through "benchmark dental benefit packages" modeled after the benchmark plans for medical services described above (e.g., dental benefit plans under FEHBP, state employee programs and commercial HMO options). The new law also includes provisions for dental education for parents of newborns and dental services through federally qualified health centers. States must report detailed information in their annual reports and for Early and Periodic Screening, Diagnostic and Treatment Services (EPSDT) reporting purposes on, for example, the number of children by age group receiving various types of dental care. Information on dental providers and covered dental services will be available to the public via the federal *Insure Kids Now* website and hotline. The child health quality improvement activities described above will include measurement of dental treatment and services to maintain dental health. GAO will conduct a study on children's access to dental care under Medicaid and CHIP. The report on this study will include recommendations for federal and state actions to address barriers to dental care, and the feasibility and appropriateness of using qualified mid-level providers to improve access.

Children who are enrolled in a group health plan or employer-sponsored health insurance are not eligible for full CHIP coverage. Under Medicaid, beneficiaries may have such private coverage. With respect to beneficiary cost-sharing, states that implement CHIP Medicaid expansions must follow the cost-sharing rules of the Medicaid program. For states that implement CHIP through a separate state program, the maximum allowable amounts vary by family income level, and aggregate cost-sharing may not exceed 5% of family income for the year.

CHIPRA also provides a state option under separate CHIP programs, subject to certain conditions, to provide dental-only supplemental coverage to children enrolled in group or employer coverage who otherwise meet CHIP eligibility criteria. The provision allows states to provide dental coverage consistent with the new dental benchmark benefits plans or cost-sharing protections for dental coverage applicable under CHIP. States may set the upper income level for this new benefit up to the level otherwise applicable under their separate CHIP programs. States are not allowed to offer dental-only supplemental coverage unless (1) the state has implemented the highest income eligibility permitted in federal CHIP statute (or a waiver) as of January 1, 2009; (2) the state does not limit acceptance of applications for children or impose any enrollment caps, waiting lists, or similar eligibility limitations under CHIP; and (3) the state provides benefits to all children in the state who apply for and meet the eligibility standards. In addition, states may not provide more favorable dental coverage or related cost-sharing protections for children provided dental-only supplemental coverage than the dental coverage or related cost-sharing protections for CHIP children eligible for the full range of CHIP benefits. States would have the option to not apply an eligibility waiting period for children provided dental-only supplemental coverage.

Section 502. Mental health parity in CHIP plans.

Medicaid and CHIP state plans may define what constitutes mental health benefits (if any). Group health plans are prohibited from imposing annual and lifetime dollar limits on mental health and substance abuse benefits that are more restrictive than those applicable to medical and surgical coverage. Similarly, group health plans may not impose more restrictive treatment limits (e.g., total outpatient hospital visits or inpatient days) or cost-sharing requirements on mental health or substance abuse coverage compared to medical and surgical services. Under Medicaid, most individuals under age 21 receive comprehensive basic screening services (i.e., well-child visits, immunizations) as well as dental, vision and hearing services, through the Early and Periodic Screening, Diagnostic and Treatment Services (EPSDT) benefit. In addition, EPSDT guarantees access to all federally coverable services necessary to treat a problem or condition among eligibles.

CHIPRA ensures that, in the case of a state CHIP plan that provides both medical and surgical benefits and mental health or substance use disorder benefits, such a plan must ensure that the financial requirements and treatment limitations applicable to such mental health or substance use disorder benefits comply with the requirements of Section 2705(a) of the Public Health Service Act in the same manner as such requirements apply to a group health plan. Generally, this means that the financial requirements and treatment limits applicable to mental health or substance use disorder benefits must be no more restrictive than the financial requirements and treatment limitations applicable to substantially all medical and surgical benefits covered under the state CHIP plan. In addition, there can be no separate cost-sharing requirements or treatment limitations applicable only to mental health or substance use disorder benefits. State CHIP plans that include coverage of EPSDT services (as defined in Medicaid statute) are deemed to satisfy this mental health parity requirement.

Section 503. Application of prospective payment system for services provided by Federally-Qualified Health Centers and Rural Health Clinics.

Under Medicaid law, payments to Federally Qualified Health Centers (FQHCs) and Rural Health Clinics (RHCs) are based on a prospective payment system. Beginning in FY2001, per visit payments were based on 100% of average costs during 1999 and 2000 adjusted for changes in the scope of services furnished. (Special rules applied to entities first established after 2000.) For subsequent years, the per visit payment for all FQHCs and RHCs equals the amounts for the preceding fiscal year increased by the percentage increase in the Medicare Economic Index applicable to primary care services, and adjusted for any changes in the scope of services furnished during that fiscal year. In managed care contracts, states are required to make supplemental payments to the facility equal to the difference between the contracted amount and the cost-based amounts.

CHIPRA requires states that operate separate and/or combination CHIP programs to reimburse FQHCs and RHCs based on the Medicaid prospective payment system. This provision applies to services provided on or after October 1, 2009. For FY2009, $5 million is appropriated (to remain available until expended) for grants to states with separate CHIP programs for expenditures related to transitioning to a prospective payment system for FQHCs/RHCs under CHIP. Finally, the Secretary is required to report to Congress (by October 1, 2011) on the effects (if any) of the new prospective payment system on access to benefits, provider payment rates, or scope of benefits.

Section 504. Premium grace period.

No statutory provision specifies a grace period for payment of CHIP premiums. Federal regulations require states' CHIP plans to describe the consequences for an enrollee or applicant who does not pay required premiums and the disenrollment protections adopted by the state. These protections must include the following: (1) the state must give enrollees reasonable notice of and an opportunity to pay past due premiums prior to disenrollment; (2) the disenrollment process must give the individual the opportunity to show a decline in family income that may qualify the individual for lower or no cost-sharing; and (3) the state must provide the enrollee with an opportunity for an impartial review to address disenrollment from the program, during which time the individual will continue to be enrolled.

CHIPRA requires states to provide CHIP enrollees with a grace period of at least 30 days from the beginning of a new coverage period to make premium payments before the individual's coverage may be terminated. Within 7 days after the first day of the grace period, the state must provide the individual with notice that failure to make a premium payment within the grace period will result in termination of coverage and that the individual has the right to challenge the proposed termination pursuant to applicable federal regulations. This provision is effective for new coverage periods beginning on or after the date of enactment of this act.

Section 505. Clarification of coverage of services provided through school-based health centers.

A number of coverable benefits are listed in the CHIP statute, such as "clinic services (including health center services) and other ambulatory health care services." CHIPRA provides that nothing in Title XXI shall be construed as limiting a state's ability to provide CHIP for covered items and services furnished through school-based health centers.

The provision also adds a definition for "school-based health center" to include a health care clinic that (1) is located in or near a school facility of a school district or board of an Indian tribe (IT) or tribal organization (TO); (2) is organized through school, community, and health provider relationships; (3) is administered by a sponsoring facility (e.g., hospital, public health department, community health center, nonprofit health care agency, school or school system, or a program administered by the Indian Health Service or Bureau of Indian Affairs, or operated by an IT or TO); (4) provides primary health services through health professionals to children in accordance with state and local law, including laws relating to licensure and certification; and (5) satisfies such other requirements as a state may establish for the operation of such a clinic.

Section 506. Medicaid and CHIP Payment and Access Commission.

CHIPRA establishes a new federal commission, called the Medicaid and CHIP Payment and Access Commission, or MACPAC. This commission will engage in a number of activities. MACPAC will review program policies under both Medicaid and CHIP affecting children's access to benefits, including (1) payment policies, including the process for updating fees for different types of providers, payment methodologies, and the impact of these factors on access and quality of care; (2) the interaction of Medicaid and CHIP payment policies with health care delivery generally; and (3) other policies, including those relating to transportation and language barriers. The commission will make recommendations to Congress concerning such access policies. Beginning in 2010, by March 1 of each year, the commission will submit a report to Congress containing the results of these reviews and MACPAC's recommendations regarding these policies. Also beginning in 2010, by June 1 of each year, the commission will submit another report to Congress containing an examination of issues affecting Medicaid and CHIP, including the implications of changes in health care delivery in the United States and in the market for health care services.

MACPAC must also create an early warning system to identify provider shortage areas or other problems that threaten access to care or the health care status of Medicaid and CHIP beneficiaries.

In addition, if the Secretary of HHS submits a report to Congress (or any such committee) that is required by law and that relates to access policies, including payment policies, under Medicaid or CHIP, a copy of that report must also be submitted to MACPAC. MACPAC will review such a report and submit written comments, along with any recommendations, to the House Committee on Energy and Commerce and the Senate Finance Committee not later than six months after the date of submittal of the Secretary's report to Congress.

MACPAC would also be required to consult periodically with the chairmen and ranking minority Members of these two congressional committees regarding MACPAC's agenda and progress toward achieving that agenda. MACPAC may conduct additional reviews, and submit additional reports to these congressional committees on such topics relating to Medicaid and CHIP as requested by such chairmen and Members, and as MACPAC deems appropriate. In addition, MACPAC must transmit to the Secretary a copy of each report submitted to Congress, and must make such reports available to the public. With respect to each recommendation made in reports by MACPAC, each commission member must vote on said recommendation, and MACPAC must include, by member, the results of that vote in the report containing that recommendation. Before making any recommendations, MACPAC must examine the budget consequences of such actions, directly or through consultation with appropriate experts.

MACPAC will be composed of 17 members appointed by the Comptroller General. Additional provisions in P.L. 111-3 further define (1) qualifications for commission members, (2) length of tenure (three years) and procedures for filling vacancies, (3) compensation for members, (4) designation of a chairman and vice chairman among members, and (5) meetings. The provision also allows the commission to establish a paid, professional staff to assist in the commission's work. MACPAC will have the power to obtain official data from any department or agency of the U.S. government that is necessary to enable it to carry out its mission. MACPAC must (1) utilize existing information where possible, collected by its own staff or under other arrangements; (2) carry out, or award grants or contracts, for original research when existing information is inadequate; and (3) adopt procedures to allow submission of information by outside parties for MACPAC's use. The Comptroller General must have unrestricted access to the work of the commission, immediately upon request, and MACPAC may be subject to periodic audits by the Comptroller General.

With respect to funding, MACPAC must submit requests for appropriations in the same manner as the Comptroller General submits such request, but amounts appropriated to MACPAC must be separate from amounts appropriated for the Comptroller General. In addition, the provision authorizes to be appropriated such sums as may be necessary to carry out the provisions of this section.

The provision also requires the Comptroller General to appoint the initial members of the commission no later than January 1, 2010. Finally, not later than January 1, 2010, and annually thereafter, the Secretary of HHS, in consultation with the Secretaries of the Treasury and Labor, and the states, must submit an annual report to Congress on the financial status of, enrollment in, and spending trends for Medicaid for the fiscal year ending on September 30 of the preceding fiscal year.

TITLE VI-PROGRAM INTEGRTITY AND OTHER MISCELLANEOUS PROVISIONS

Subtitle A-Program Integrity and Data Collection.

Section 601. Payment error rate measurement ("PERM").

Federal agencies are required to annually review programs that are susceptible to significant erroneous payments, and to estimate the amount of improper payments, to report those estimates to Congress, and to submit a report on actions the agency is taking to reduce erroneous payments. On August 21, 2007, CMS issued a final rule for PERM for Medicaid and CHIP (effective October 1, 2007) which responded to comments received on a interim final rule, and included some changes to that interim final rule. Assessments of payment error rates related to claims for both fee-for-service and managed care services, as well as eligibility determinations are made. A predecessor to PERM, called the Medicaid Eligibility Quality Control (MEQC) system, is operated by state Medicaid agencies for similar purposes.

CHIPRA includes a number of detailed requirements with respect to the applicability of PERM requirements to CHIP. For example, the provision requires that the final PERM rule include (1) clearly defined criteria for errors for both states and providers, (2) a clearly defined process for appealing error determinations by review contractors, and (3) clearly defined responsibilities and deadlines for states implementing corrective action plans. The new law also requires the Secretary to review the MEQC requirements with the PERM requirements and coordinate consistent implementation of both sets of requirements, while reducing redundancies. The Secretary is also required to establish state-specific sample sizes for application of PERM requirements to CHIP. This activity would begin with the first fiscal year that begins on or after the date on which the new final rule is in effect for all states. In establishing such sample sizes, the Secretary must minimize the administrative cost burden on states under Medicaid and CHIP, and must maintain state flexibility to manage these programs. The new final rule must be promulgated not later than six months after the enactment of CHIPRA. Finally, the new law applies a federal matching rate of 90% to expenditures related to administration of PERM requirements applicable to CHIP. The provision also excludes from the 10% cap on CHIP administrative expenses all expenditures related to administration of PERM requirements applicable to CHIP.

Section 602. Improving data collection.

Under prior law, the Secretary of Commerce was required to make appropriate adjustments to the Current Population Survey (CPS), which is the primary data source for determining states' current law CHIP allotments, (1) to produce statistically reliable annual state data on the number of low-income children who do not have health insurance coverage; (2) to produce data that categorizes such children by family income, age, and race or ethnicity; and (3) where appropriate, to expand the sample size used in the state sampling units, to expand the number of sampling units in a state, and to include an appropriate verification element. For this purpose, $10 million was appropriated annually, beginning in FY2000.

CHIPRA provides $20 million for FY2009 and each subsequent year thereafter to produce these data for CHIP purposes. In addition to the prior-law requirements of the appropriation, for data collection beginning with FY2009, in consultation with the Secretary of HHS, the Secretary of Commerce is required to (1) make adjustments to the CPS to develop more accurate state-specific estimates of the number of children enrolled in CHIP or Medicaid, (2) make adjustments to the CPS to improve the survey estimates used to determine the child population growth factor in the new financing structure under CHIPRA and any other necessary data, (3) include health insurance survey information for the American Community Survey (ACS) related to children, and (4) assess whether estimates from the ACS produce more reliable estimates than the CPS for the child population growth factor in the new CHIP financing structure established under this new law. On the basis of that assessment, the Commerce Secretary will recommend to the HHS Secretary whether ACS estimates should be used in lieu of, or in some combination with, CPS estimates for these purposes. If such a recommendation is made, a period for transition may be established and implemented in a manner designed to avoid adverse impacts on states.

Section 603. Updated Federal evaluation of CHIP.

The Secretary of HHS was required to conduct an independent evaluation of 10 states with approved CHIP plans, and to submit a report on that study to Congress by December 31, 2001. Ten million dollars was appropriated for this purpose in FY2000 and was available for expenditure through FY2002. The 10 states chosen for the evaluation were to be ones that utilized diverse approaches to providing CHIP coverage, represented various geographic areas (including a mix of rural and urban areas), and contained a significant portion of uninsured children. A number of matters were included in this evaluation, including (1) surveys of the target populations; (2) an evaluation of effective and ineffective outreach and enrollment strategies, and identification of enrollment barriers; (3) the extent to which coordination between Medicaid and CHIP affected enrollment; (4) an assessment of the effects of cost-sharing on utilization, enrollment and retention; and (5) an evaluation of disenrollment or other retention issues.

CHIPRA requires the Secretary of HHS to conduct a new, independent federal evaluation of 10 states with approved CHIP plans, directly or through contracts or interagency agreements, as before. The new evaluation must be submitted to Congress by December 31, 2011. Ten million dollars would be appropriated for this purpose in FY2010 and made available for expenditure through FY2012. The prior-law language for the types of states to be chosen and the matters included in the evaluation also apply to this new evaluation.

Section 604. Access to records for IG and GAO audits and evaluations.

Every third fiscal year (beginning with FY2000), the Secretary (through the Inspector General of the Department of Health and Human Services) must audit a sample from among the states with an approved CHIP state plan that does not, as a part of that plan, provide health benefits coverage under Medicaid. The Comptroller General of the United States must monitor these audits and, not later than March 1 of each fiscal year after a fiscal year in which an audit is conducted, submit a report to Congress on the results of the audit conducted during the prior fiscal year.

Under CHIPRA, for the purpose of evaluating and auditing CHIP (both separate CHIP programs and Medicaid expansions under CHIP), the Secretary, the Office of Inspector General, and the Comptroller General must have access to any books, accounts, records, correspondence, and other documents that are related to the expenditure of federal CHIP funds and that are in the possession, custody, or control of states, political subdivisions of states, or their grantees or contractors.

Section 605. No Federal funding for illegal aliens; disallowance for unauthorized expenditures.

CHIPRA restates prior law that federal funding for individuals who are not lawfully residing in the United States is not allowed, and that the law provides for the disallowance of federal funding of erroneous expenditures under Medicaid and CHIP.

Subtitle B-Miscellaneous Health Provisions

Section 611. Deficit Reduction Act technical corrections.

Under the Early and Periodic Screening, Diagnostic and Treatment (EPSDT) benefit under Medicaid, most individuals under age 21 must have access to comprehensive basic screening services (e.g., well-child visits including age-appropriate immunizations) as well as dental, vision, and hearing services. In addition, EPSDT guarantees access to all federally coverable services necessary to treat a problem or condition among eligible individuals.

The Deficit Reduction Act of 2005 (DRA; P.L. 109-171) gave states the option to provide Medicaid to state-specified groups through enrollment in benchmark and benchmark-equivalent coverage that is nearly identical to plans available under SCHIP. This law identified a number of groups as exempt from mandatory enrollment in benchmark or benchmark-equivalent plans. These groups may be enrolled in such plans on a voluntary basis. One such exempted group was children in foster care receiving child welfare services under Part B of title IV of the Social Security Act and children receiving foster care or adoption assistance under Part E of such title. For any child under age 19 in one of the major mandatory and optional eligibility groups in Medicaid, wrap-around benefits to the DRA benchmark and benchmark-equivalent coverage include EPSDT.

The provision in CHIPRA identifies specific sections of prior Medicaid law (instead of all of Title XIX as specified in DRA) that will be disregarded in order to provide benchmark benefit coverage. It also specifies that an individual's entitlement to EPSDT services remains intact under the benchmark benefit package option under DRA. The provision also makes a correction to the reference to children in foster care receiving child welfare services in P.L. 109-171. Lastly, the provision requires the Secretary of HHS to publish on the CMS internet website the list of provisions in Title XIX that do not apply in order to enable a state to provide benchmark coverage under Medicaid on the date that such approval is given (rather than within 30 days of such approval). It also requires the Secretary to publish these same findings in the *Federal Register* within 30 days of the date of approval. The effective date of these provisions is the same as the original DRA provision (i.e., March 31, 2006).

Section 612. References to title XXI.

A provision in P.L. 106-113 directed the Secretary of HHS or any other federal officer or employee, with respect to references to the program under Title XXI, in any publication or official communication, to use the term "SCHIP" instead of "CHIP" and to use the term "State children's health insurance program" instead of "children's health insurance program." A provision in CHIPRA repeals this section of P.L. 106-113.

Section 613. Prohibiting initiation of new health opportunity account demonstration programs.

The Deficit Reduction Act of 2005 allowed the Secretary of HHS to establish no more than 10 demonstration programs within Medicaid for Health Opportunity Accounts (HOAs). HOAs were used to pay (via electronic funds transfers) health care expenses specified by the state. CHIPRA prohibits the Secretary of HHS from approving any new Health Opportunity Account demonstrations as of February 4, 2009.

Section 614. Adjustment in computation of Medicaid FMAP to disregard an extraordinary employer pension contribution.

The federal medical assistance percentage (FMAP) is the rate at which states are reimbursed for most Medicaid service expenditures. It is based on a formula that provides higher reimbursement to states with lower per capita incomes relative to the national average (and vice versa). When state FMAPs are calculated by HHS for the upcoming fiscal year, the state and U.S. per capita income amounts used in the formula are equal to the average of the three most recent calendar years of data on per capita personal income available from the Department of Commerce's Bureau of Economic Analysis (BEA). BEA revises its most recent estimates of state per capita personal income on an annual basis to incorporate revised and newly available source data on population and income. It also undertakes a comprehensive data revision every few years that may result in upward and downward revisions to each of the component parts of personal income, one of which is employer contributions for employee pension and insurance funds. In describing its 2003 comprehensive revision, BEA reported that upward revisions to employer contributions for pensions beginning with 1989 were the result of methodological improvements and more complete source data.

A provision in CHIPRA makes an adjustment in the computation of Medicaid FMAP to disregard an extraordinary employer pension contribution. For the purposes of computing Medicaid FMAPs beginning with FY2006, any significantly disproportionate employer pension or insurance fund contribution will be disregarded in computing state per capita income, but not U.S. per capita income. A significantly disproportionate employer pension and insurance fund contribution is defined as any identifiable employer contribution towards pension or other employee insurance funds that is estimated to accrue to residents of such state for a calendar year (beginning with calendar year 2003) if the increase in the amount so estimated exceeds 25% of the total increase in personal income in that state for the year involved. For estimating and adjusting an FMAP already calculated as of the date of enactment for a state with a significantly disproportionate employer pension and insurance fund contribution, the Secretary must use the personal income data set originally used in calculating such FMAP. If in any calendar year the total personal income growth in a state is negative, an employer pension and insurance fund contribution for the purposes of calculating the state's FMAP for a calendar year shall not exceed 125% of the amount of such contribution for the previous calendar year for the state. No state would have its FMAP for a fiscal year reduced as a result of the application of this provision. Not later than May 15, 2009, the Secretary must submit to the Congress a report on the problems presented by the current treatment of pension and insurance fund contributions in the use of Bureau of Economic Affairs calculations for the FMAP and for Medicaid and on possible alternative methodologies to mitigate such problems.

Section 615. Clarification treatment of regional medical center.

The states and federal government share in the cost of the Medicaid program. Sometimes hospitals fund the state share of some of its own Medicaid payments, thereby ensuring that federal matching funds will be available even if the state cannot pay its share. Such "intergovernmental transfers" of certified public expenditures made by those types of health care providers to fund the non-federal share of states' Medicaid expenditures are allowable but only under certain circumstances. Some of those circumstances are described in detailed federal regulations. Other limitations are based on recent CMS administrative actions. For example, CMS has denied federal matching payments when the state share was comprised of payments transferred from out-of-state hospitals.

A provision in CHIPRA prohibits the Secretary from denying federal matching payments when the state share has been transferred from or certified by a publicly owned regional medical center located in another state (and meeting certain additional criteria identified below) if the Secretary determines that the use of such funds is proper and in the interest of the Medicaid program. Such a publicly owned regional center (1) provides level 1 trauma and burn care services; (2) provides level 3 neonatal services; (3) is obligated to serve all patients, regardless of ability to pay; (4) is located within an SMSA that includes at least 3 states; (5) provides services as a tertiary care provider for patients residing within a 125-mile radius; and (6) meets Medicaid's disproportionate share hospital definition in at least one state other than the state in which it is located.

Section 616. Extension of Medicaid DSH allotments for Tennessee and Hawaii.

When establishing hospital payment rates, state Medicaid programs are required to recognize the situation of hospitals that provide a disproportionate share of care to low-income patients with special needs. Such "disproportionate share hospital (DSH) payments" are subject to statewide allotment caps. Allotments for Tennessee and Hawaii, however, are equal to zero because the states operate their state Medicaid programs under the provisions of a Section 1115 research and demonstration waiver. Such waivers allow for states to waive various provisions of Medicaid law specified in Title XIX (such as the requirement to make DSH payments) to conduct demonstrations as long as the demonstrations are likely to assist in promoting the objectives of the Medicaid program. Congress has enacted special DSH provisions for Tennessee and Hawaii in the past. Tennessee's allotments were set at $30 million for each of FY2007 through FY2009, and one-quarter of that amount was made available for the first quarter of FY2010. Hawaii's allotments were also set at $10 million for each of FY2007 through FY2009, and $2.5 million was made available for the first quarter of FY2010. Both states have, in addition, been allowed to submit state plan amendments describing their methodologies for distributing such payments for the Secretary's approval.

A provision in CHIPRA extends the special DSH allotment arrangements for Tennessee and Hawaii through a portion of FY2012. Allotment amounts would be equal to $30 million for Tennessee for each full fiscal year—2010 and 2011—and one-quarter of that amount would be available for the first quarter of FY2012. Hawaii's $10 allotment would be extended for each full fiscal year—2010 and 2011—and $2.5 million would be available for the first quarter of FY2012.

Section 617. GAO report on Medicaid managed care payment rates.

A provision in CHIPRA requires GAO to submit a report to the Senate Finance Committee and the House Energy and Commerce Committee that analyzes the extent to which state payment rates for Medicaid managed care organizations are actuarially sound. This report will be due not later than 18 months after the date of enactment of this act.

Subtitle C-Other Provisions

Section 621. Outreach regarding health insurance options available to children.

CHIPRA establishes a task force, consisting of the Administrator of the Small Business Administration (SBA) and the Secretaries of HHS, Labor, and the Treasury, to conduct a nationwide campaign of education and outreach for small businesses regarding the availability of coverage for children through private insurance, Medicaid, and CHIP. The campaign includes information regarding options to make insurance more affordable, including federal and state tax deductions and credits and the federal tax exclusion available under employer-sponsored cafeteria plans; it also includes efforts to educate small businesses about the value of health insurance coverage for children, assistance available through public programs, and the availability of the hotline operated as part of the Insure Kids Now program at HHS. The task force will be allowed to use any business partner of the SBA, enter into a memorandum of understanding with a chamber of commerce and a partnership with any appropriate small business or health advocacy group, and designate outreach programs at HHS regional offices to work with SBA district offices. It requires the SBA website to prominently display links to state eligibility and enrollment requirements for Medicaid and CHIP, and requires a report to Congress every two years.

Section 622. Sense of the Senate regarding access to affordable and meaningful health insurance coverage.

CHIPRA establishes a Sense of the Senate—The Senate finds the following: (1) there are approximately 45 million Americans currently without health insurance; (2) more than half of uninsured workers are employed by businesses with less than 25 employees or are self-employed; (3) health insurance premiums continue to rise at more than twice the rate of inflation for all consumer goods; (4) individuals in the small group and individual health insurance markets usually pay more for similar coverage than those in the large group market; and (5) the rapid growth in health insurance costs over the last few years has forced many employers, particularly small employers, to increase deductibles and co-pays or to drop coverage completely.

The Senate (1) recognizes the necessity to improve affordability and access to health insurance for all Americans; (2) acknowledges the value of building upon the existing private health insurance market; and (3) affirms its intent to enact legislation this year that, with appropriate protection for consumers, improves access to affordable and meaningful health insurance coverage for employees of small businesses and individuals by—(A) facilitating pooling mechanisms, including pooling across State lines; and (B) providing assistance to small businesses and individuals, including financial assistance and tax incentives, for the purchase of private insurance coverage.

TITLE VII-REVENUE PROVISIONS

Section 701. Increase in excise tax rate under tobacco products.

The source of revenue for CHIPRA would be an increase in tobacco excise taxes. The vast majority of tobacco taxes are on cigarettes, which account for 97% of federal tobacco tax revenue. Under prior law, excise taxes on cigarettes and other tobacco products included the following rates:

- federal cigarette taxes: $0.39 per pack;

- small cigars: $.04 per package of 20;

- large cigars: 20.719% of sales price, not to exceed $48.75 per 1,000 units (i.e., a maximum tax of almost $.05 per cigar);

- chewing tobacco: $.01 per ounce;

- snuff: $.04 per ounce; and

- pipe and roll-your-own tobacco: $.07 per ounce.

There are also taxes on cigarette paper and cigarette tubes. These taxes are imposed per pound and under prior law the rates were as follows: (1) $0.195 for chewing tobacco, (2) $0.585 for snuff, and (3) $1.0606 for pipe and roll-your-own tobacco. There are also taxes on large cigarettes that are essentially non-existent (although a tax is necessary for administrative reasons).

CHIPRA increases taxes on cigarettes and tobacco-related products (effective April 1, 2009) to the following rates:

- federal cigarette taxes would be increased to $1.0066 per pack;

- small cigars would have their taxes increased to the same level as cigarettes;

- large cigars would be subject to a tax of 52.75% of sales price with a maximum of $0.4026 per cigar;

- chewing tobacco would be increased to approximately $.03 per ounce (and $0.5033 per pound);

- snuff would be increased to $.09 per ounce ($1.51 per pound);

- pipe tobacco would be increased to $.18 per ounce ($2.8311 per pound);

- roll-your-own tobacco would be increased to $1.55 per ounce ($24.78 per pound);

- cigarette papers taxes would rise from $1.22 per 40, to $3.15;

- cigarette tubes would rise from $2.44 to $6.30.

CHIPRA also includes provisions affecting floor stock taxes that would apply to items removed from the manufacturer before the April 1, 2009, effective date, and subsequently sold after that date. The person holding the items on April 1, 2009, will be liable, and there will be a $500 credit per person. (A person is considered to be a controlled group. For example, a corporation can not receive the $500 credit for each of its subsidiaries.) The floor stocks tax will also apply to products in a foreign trade zone (i.e., imports). The purpose of the floor stock tax will be to prevent the stockpiling of tobacco products before April 1, 2009, the effective date for future sales.

Section 702. Administrative improvements.

CHIPRA imposes regulatory and reporting requirements on manufacturers and importers of processed tobacco other than the tobacco products subject to excise taxes, and expands the definition of roll–your-own tobacco to include tobacco that could be used to make cigars.

Section 703. Treasury study concerning magnitude of tobacco smuggling in the United States.

CHIPRA expands the scope of penalties for not paying the tobacco-related tax, clarifies the statute of limitations, and mandates a study of tobacco smuggling.

Section 704. Time for payment of corporate estimated taxes.

Under prior law, quarterly estimated corporate tax payments due in July, August, and September of 2013 are 120% of the normal required payment, with the next such payment reduced accordingly. CHIPRA increases the ratio to 120.5% and shifts $300 million of corporate taxes from FY2014 to FY2013. The prior-law 120% withholding provision does not apply to firms with assets of less than $1 billion, and the withholding increase under CHIPRA will not alter that exemption.

Appendix. A Summary of Major CHIP Legislation During the 110th and 111th Congresses[9]

During the 110th Congress, a number of CHIP bills saw legislative action. A majority of the CHIP changes enacted in public laws included provisions to add additional appropriations to CHIP, but did not make any major substantive changes to the program.[10] The 110th Congress enacted provisions to

- address certain states' shortfalls in FY2007 federal CHIP funding (U.S. Troop Readiness, Veterans' Care, Katrina Recovery, and Iraq Accountability Appropriations Act, 2007, P.L. 110-28);

- provide temporary FY2008 appropriations for CHIP through December 31, 2007 through continuing resolutions (P.L. 110-92, P.L. 110-116, P.L. 110-137, P.L. 110-149); and

- provide additional appropriations through March 31, 2009 (The Medicare, Medicaid, and CHIP Extension Act of 2007, P.L. 110-173).

The 110th Congress also considered CHIP reauthorization legislation that would have made important changes to Medicaid and CHIP. Numerous bills were introduced, and two that were passed by Congress (H.R. 976 and H.R. 3963) were vetoed by President Bush. **Table A-1** includes a timeline of the legislative floor action on the major CHIP reauthorization bills during the 110th and 111th Congresses.

---

[9] During the 112th Congress, The American Taxpayer Relief Act (ATRA, P.L. 112-240) extended the state option for "Express Lane" eligibility determinations for Medicaid and CHIP children through September 30, 2014. No other legislative changes were made to the CHIP program during the 112th Congress.

[10] A complete legislative history of the CHIP program is contained in CRS Congressional Distribution Memorandum CHIP Legislative History, by Elicia J. Herz and Chris L. Peterson, available upon request.

Table A-1. Timeline of Legislative Floor Action
on the Major CHIP Reauthorization Bills

| Bill | | House Vote (result) | Senate Vote (result) | Conference | | Presidential Action (result) | House Override (result)a |
Name	Number			House (result)	Senate (result)		
110th Congress							
CHAMPb	H.R. 3162	8/1/2007 (225-204)					
CHIPRA Ic	H.R. 976		8/2/2007 (68-31)	9/25/2007 (265-159)	9/27/2007 (67-29)	10/3/07 (veto)	10/18/2007 (273-156)
CHIPRA II	H.R. 3963	10/25/2007 (265-142)	11/1/2007 (64-30)			12/12/07 (veto)	1/23/2008 (260-152)
111th Congress							
CHIPRA (2009)	H.R. 2	1/14/2009 (289-139)					
CHIPRA (2009)	H.R. 2 (as amended by the Senate)	2/04/2009 (290-135)	1/29/2009 (66-32)			2/4/2009 (P.L. 111-3)	

Source: Prepared by the Congressional Research Service.

a. Two-thirds majority required for veto override. Both votes were short of that margin.

b. Children's Health and Medicare Protection Act of 2007 (CHAMP).

c. Children's Health Insurance Program Reauthorization Act of 2007 (also referred to as CHIPRA I or S. 1893/H.R. 976).

Overview of the Vetoed H.R. 3963 and H.R. 976

The 110th Congress's H.R. 976 (CHIPRA I) and H.R. 3963 (CHIPRA II) shared many common elements, including

- national allotment appropriations totaling $61.4 billion over five years (which represented an increase of $36.2 billion over the prior law baseline of $25.2 billion), distributed to states and territories using a new formula primarily based on their past and/or projected federal CHIP spending;

- a new contingency fund (for making payments to states for certain shortfalls of federal CHIP funds), which would have received deposits through a separate appropriation each year through FY2012 and made payments of up to 20% of the available national allotment for CHIP;

- new performance bonus payments (for states exceeding certain child enrollment levels and states that implement certain outreach and enrollment initiatives), which were to be funded with an FY2008 appropriation of $3 billion and deposits of certain unspent CHIP funds through FY2012;

- additional grants for outreach and enrollment that would have totaled $100 million each year through FY2012;

- provisions to remove barriers to enrollment;

- provisions related to benefits (e.g., dental, mental health, and Early and Periodic, Screening, Diagnosis and Treatment [EPSDT]);

- provisions to eliminate barriers to providing premium assistance;

- provisions to strengthen quality of care and health outcomes of children;

- program integrity and miscellaneous provisions, including some that affect the Medicaid program; and

- tobacco tax changes.

Cost estimates from the Congressional Budget Office (CBO) indicated that H.R. 976 would have increased outlays by $34.9 billion over 5 years and by $71.5 billion over 10 years,[11] and H.R. 3963 would have increased outlays by $35.4 billion over 5 years and by $71.5 billion over 10 years.[12] Costs in both bills would have been offset by an increase in the federal tobacco tax (mostly from an increase in the federal tax by 61 cents per pack of cigarettes) and other changes, which the Joint Committee on Taxation (JCT) estimated would have increased on-budget revenue by $35.5 billion over 5 years and by $71.7 billion over 10 years.

On any given day in 2007, approximately 9 million children were without health insurance. Most of these children came from two-parent families (53%). Most had a parent who worked full time all year (60%).[13] And other data indicate most uninsured children are *eligible* for Medicaid or CHIP (62%).[14] According to the Congressional Budget Office (CBO), the two vetoed CHIPRA bills both would have increased average monthly FY2012 Medicaid and CHIP enrollment by 5.8 million, for a total of 34.1 million projected enrollees. In both bills, about 80% of the increased enrollment would have occurred among current eligibility groups, rather than new ones.[15]

Author Contact Information

Evelyne P. Baumrucker
Analyst in Health Care Financing
ebaumrucker@crs.loc.gov, 7-8913

Elicia J. Herz
Specialist in Health Care Financing
eherz@crs.loc.gov, 7-1377

Jane G. Gravelle
Senior Specialist in Economic Policy
jgravelle@crs.loc.gov, 7-7829

---

[11] CBO, letter to the Honorable John Dingell (September 25, 2007), available at http://www.cbo.gov/ftpdocs/86xx/doc8655/hr976.pdf.

[12] CBO, CBO's Estimate of the Effects on Direct Spending and Revenues of the Children's Health Insurance Program (October 24, 2007), available at http://www.cbo.gov/ftpdocs/87xx/doc8741/hr976DingellLtr10-24-2007.pdf.

[13] CRS Report 97-975, *Health Insurance Coverage of Children, 2008*.

[14] Julie L. Hudson and Thomas M. Selden, "Children's Eligibility And Coverage: Recent Trends And A Look Ahead," Health Affairs Web exclusive, August 16, 2007, pp. w618-629.

[15] Previously cited CBO cost estimates.

Acknowledgments

The authors wish to thank Chris L. Peterson, former CRS Specialist in Health Care Financing, who co-authored the original report.